Promoting Entry By Troops

A Statement and Compilation Prepared by the Research Department
of the Universal House of Justice

October 1993

Bahá'í Publications Australia

ISBN 0 909991 66 9

3rd Printing 1994

Printed and bound by Daram Printing Pty Ltd, Seven Hills NSW 2147, Australia

Table of Contents

THE UNIVERSAL HOUSE OF JUSTICE
BAHÁ'Í WORLD CENTRE
9 November 1993

To all National Spiritual Assemblies

Beloved Friends,

In the message sent last Ridván, we drew the attention of the Bahá'í world to the critical need for a massive expansion of the Bahá'í community in the years immediately ahead. The growing receptivity of the peoples of the world to Bahá'u'lláh's Message reinforces our conviction that entry by troops will soon become an established pattern for the growth of the Faith in country after country.

To assist the National Spiritual Assemblies and all the friends to understand, welcome, initiate and sustain this process, we are enclosing a compilation entitled "Promoting Entry by Troops" and a covering statement prepared by the Research Department. Whoever studies these illuminating passages will perceive that entry by troops is not merely a stage of the progress of the Cause destined to occur in its own good time, dependent on the receptivity of the population as a whole — it is a phenomenon which the Bahá'í communities, by their own activities, can prepare for and help to bring about. It is also a process which, once started, can be sustained. By a wise allocation of resources and the energetic pursuit of simultaneous plans of expansion, deepening and consolidation, the process of entry by troops should bring about a rapidly increasing supply of active believers, soundly based local communities, and steadily evolving local and national Bahá'í institutions.

The Bahá'í world needs to foster a united clarity of vision for the expansion of the Cause and all its agencies, and a wide range of activities suited to the differing conditions of both the general population and the individual Bahá'ís. We therefore urge the friends, and especially the Assemblies, to study this compilation, to understand the coherence of its statements, and to use its counsels to

"

lend a renewed impetus to the spread of the Faith and the establishment of the institutions of the Cause of God.

Above all, in every aspect of teaching the Message, the friends should have confidence in the regenerative power of the Word of God, seek strength from the hosts of divine assistance, and anticipate the bounties that will continually be showered upon them. To build a new world is no easy task. The road is stony and filled with obstacles, but the journey is infinitely rewarding.

It is our ardent prayer at the Sacred Threshold that the friends throughout the world, with their hearts filled with love for Bahá'u'lláh, will arise to teach His Message to the thirsting multitudes, and will welcome into His Cause all those whose spirits respond to the Divine Summons and who are moved to throw in their lot with the builders of God's Kingdom on this earth.

We are confident that, guided and assisted by the Counsellors and their auxiliaries, you will be confirmed in your efforts to direct the energies of the friends towards this momentous undertaking.

With loving Bahá'í greetings,

The Universal House of Justice

PROMOTING ENTRY BY TROOPS

A Statement Prepared by the Research Department of the
Universal House of Justice
October 1993

Shoghi Effendi's vision of the organic unfoldment of the Faith shapes our perception of the glorious future possibilities in the teaching field. In a letter addressed to the American believers in 1953 where he points to the need for deploying pioneers, the beloved Guardian states that "a steady flow of reinforcements" will

> presage and hasten the advent of the day which, as prophesied by 'Abdu'l-Bahá, will witness the entry by troops of peoples of divers nations and races into the Bahá'í world — a day which, viewed in its proper perspective, will be the prelude to that long-awaited hour when mass conversion on the part of these same nations and races, and as a direct result of a chain of events, momentous and possibly catastrophic in nature ..., will suddenly revolutionize the fortunes of the Faith, derange the equilibrium of the world, and reinforce a thousandfold the numerical strength as well as the material power and the spiritual authority of the Faith of Bahá'u'lláh.[1]

Writing in its 1990 Ridván message, the Universal House of Justice links the "increasing instances of entry by troops" in different parts of the world to the developmental stages described by Shoghi Effendi. It also fixes our place in this historical process and challenges the believers to action. The House of Justice attests:

> We have every encouragement to believe that large-scale enrolments will expand, involving village after village, town after town, from one country to another. However, it is not for us to wait passively for the ultimate fulfilment of Shoghi Effendi's vision. We few, placing our whole trust in the providence of God and regarding as a divine privilege the challenges which face us, must proceed to victory with the plans in hand.[2]

To assist the friends in refining their understanding of the processes associated with entry by troops and in responding to the challenge posed by the House of Justice we attach a compilation of extracts from letters written by or on behalf of Shoghi Effendi and the Universal House of Justice, and we offer the following comments aimed at exploring and highlighting some of the themes drawn from the compilation. In sections 1 and 2 of this statement, we describe a number of general features of the growth process and call attention to factors that contribute to the expansion of the Faith, while, in section 3, we focus on specific activities that can be undertaken to promote and sustain the process of entry by troops.

1. Some Characteristics of Growth

Before considering the subject of entry by troops we begin by examining a number of general features associated with the processes by which the Bahá'í Faith grows.

1.1 Organic Growth

The growth of the Faith proceeds in an organic, evolutionary manner.[3] Its rate of growth is, therefore, not necessarily uniform,[4] rather, it advances "in vast surges, precipitated by the alternation of crisis and victory".[5] Shoghi Effendi has also stated that the spread of the Faith all over the world will be accompanied by an acceleration of its rate of growth.[6]

For the present, the Faith is not growing at the same rate throughout the world. The Universal House of Justice has observed that there is an "eager receptivity" to the Faith in many lands,[7] and that certain segments of the population may, initially, tend to be more responsive than others to the Cause.[8] In those areas where the receptivity is just beginning to dawn, the House of Justice counsels the believers to have confidence that "the time is coming when the number of their fellow-countrymen who accept the Faith will suddenly increase".[9]

With regard to the immediate future, the Universal House of Justice affirms that the rate of growth is destined to accelerate. It states that "the stage is set for universal, rapid and massive growth of the

Cause",[10] and it envisages that all national communities will reap the harvest of entry by troops.[11]

1.2 Dynamic of Crisis and Victory

The dynamic interplay of the processes of crisis and victory characterizes the development of the Faith.[12] Shoghi Effendi affirms that "the record of its tumultuous history" demonstrates

> the supreme truth that with every fresh outbreak of hostility to the Faith, whether from within or from without, a corresponding measure of outpouring grace, sustaining its defenders and confounding its adversaries, has been providentially released, communicating a fresh impulse to the onward march of the Faith, while this impetus, in its turn, would, through its manifestations, provoke fresh hostility in quarters heretofore unaware of its challenging implications...[13]

The Universal House of Justice, likewise, allies the continuing emergence of the Faith from obscurity and the maturation of the functioning of the administrative institutions with the community's response to the recent wave of persecutions in Iran[14] and it foreshadows that "the present victories will lead to active opposition".[15]

1.3 Impact of Social Decline

Shoghi Effendi calls attention to the purifying influence of suffering and tribulation, associated with the process of social decline, on the expansion of the Faith.[16] And, in a letter written on his behalf, the Guardian notes that "after mankind has suffered ... people will enter the Cause of God in troops".[17]

The Universal House of Justice graphically depicts the impact of the declining process on humanity, relates it to mankind's spiritual search[18] and underlines the pressing responsibility of the Bahá'ís, both to increase the tempo of their teaching activities,[19] "lest opportunity be lost in the swiftly changing moods of a frenetic world",[20] and to create the kind of community that offers such a distinctive pattern of life that it will "rekindle hope among the increasingly disillusioned members of society".[21]

1.4 Emergence from Obscurity

The progress of the Faith is hastened by the opportunities afforded by its emergence from obscurity. The Universal House of Justice refers to "the emergence of a new paradigm of opportunity for further growth and consolidation of our world-wide community",[22] and it underlines the urgent challenge facing the Bahá'í community to meet the needs of the possibilities that arise as the Lesser Peace approaches.[23]

2. Factors Contributing to Growth

By way of introduction, it is important to observe that the beloved Guardian, in a letter dated 18 February 1932 written on his behalf, underscores the fact that a mere increase in the number of believers does not necessarily connote progress of the Cause. He states:

> It is not sufficient to number the souls that embrace the Cause to know the progress that it is making. The more important consequences of your activities are the spirit that is diffused into the life of the community, and the extent to which the teachings we proclaim become part of the consciousness and belief of the people that hear them. For it is only when the spirit has thoroughly permeated the world that the people will begin to enter the Faith in large numbers.[24]

Likewise, in the 1989 Riḍván message, the Universal House of Justice affirms:

> It is not enough to proclaim the Bahá'í message, essential as that is. It is not enough to expand the rolls of Bahá'í membership, vital as that is. Souls must be transformed, communities thereby consolidated, new models of life thus attained. Transformation is the essential purpose of the Cause of Bahá'u'lláh, but it lies in the will and effort of the individual to achieve it in obedience to the Covenant.[25]

From a study of the letters of Shoghi Effendi and the Universal House of Justice it is possible to identify several factors that contribute to the large-scale growth of the Faith. These factors interact with and reinforce each other and, when they operate in concert, they provide the basis for the creation of a growth-producing milieu—a Bahá'í community whose members are dedicated to refining their understanding of the nature of teaching and to learning how to work together in ways that will both accelerate and sustain the processes of expansion and consolidation. Included among these interactive factors are the following.

2.1 Commitment to Spiritual Transformation

The crucial link between individual transformation and the gradual maturation of the functioning of the Bahá'í community and the growth of the Faith is a familiar theme in the letters of Shoghi Effendi and the Universal House of Justice. Fostering such transformation in personal and family life, in the functioning of communities and Assemblies is the responsibility of individuals[26] and Bahá'í institutions, alike.[27] As Shoghi Effendi explains:

> When the true spirit of teaching, which calls for complete dedication, consecration to the noble mission, and living the life, is fulfilled, not only by the individuals, but by the Assemblies also, then the Faith will grow by leaps and bounds.[28]

2.2 Love and Unity

Love and unity among the believers[29] and love of the friends for the Faith and its institutions[30] are fundamental to attracting large numbers of people to the Cause. The beloved Guardian describes unity and love among the friends as "the spirit which must animate their Community life",[31] and he spells out their practical implications in relation to the planning and implementation of the teaching work. In a letter written on his behalf, he guides the believers as follows:

> Let them put more effort into perfecting their purely Bahá'í relationships, become more united, more spiritually

educated, more skilled in fulfilling their administrative tasks, as a preparation to teaching and welcoming larger numbers of new believers.[32]

The Universal House of Justice calls attention to another important aspect of this subject. It cautions against the polarization of views about teaching methods and approaches, and offers the following advice to the believers:

> In this, as in all aspects of the work of the Cause, the solution lies in the friends' being patient and forbearing towards those whose shortcomings distress them, and in endeavouring, through the Assemblies' consultation, to draw closer to a proper balance while maintaining the momentum of the work and canalizing the enthusiasm of the believers.[33]

2.3 Universal Participation

Universal participation and persistent efforts by the friends to teach the Cause, to apply its principles, and to further the development of its institutions are not only "indispensable to developing the human resources necessary to the progress of the Cause"[34] but they also enhance success in teaching.[35]

2.4 Balance Between Expansion and Consolidation

The Universal House of Justice refers to expansion and consolidation as "twin processes that must go hand in hand".[36] It states that they are "inseparable processes",[37] and that they represent "the primary objectives of teaching".[38] Stressing the relationship between consolidation and teaching, the House of Justice in a letter written on its behalf stated:

> Proper consolidation is essential to the preservation of the spiritual health of the community, to the protection of its interests, to the upholding of its good name, and ultimately to the continuation of the work of expansion itself.[39]

2.5 Bahá'í Community as a Model

The Bahá'í community and the Administrative Order must continue to be developed and presented to the world as a viable model and an alternative means of social organization. This is an ongoing process. Shoghi Effendi, in a letter written on his behalf, attests that:

> Until the public sees in the Bahá'í Community a true pattern, in action, of something better than it already has, it will not respond to the Faith in large numbers.[40]

In like manner, the Universal House of Justice calls attention to the distinctiveness of the Bahá'í community and states that, as the contrast between the community and the world at large increases, it "must eventually attract the disillusioned masses and cause them to enter the haven of the Covenant of Bahá'u'lláh".[41] Further, the House of Justice notes that there is increasing concern about the affairs of mankind and the inability of the old order to solve critical social problems. Since the Bahá'í Administrative Order is designed to be a pattern for future society, there is a pressing need to demonstrate "the potentialities inherent in the administrative system" and to provide, thereby, "a signal of hope to those who despair".[42]

Given the close relationships between elements of growth described above and their interactive nature, it is suggested that while each factor contributes to the expansion process, no one factor, by itself, would appear to be sufficient to produce and sustain large-scale enrolments. To concentrate on one to the exclusion of the others may well distort the teaching process and retard the long-term growth and expansion of the Bahá'í community. Further, Shoghi Effendi affirms that engagement in the teaching work reinforces the development of the very factors that contribute to the growth of the Faith. In a letter written on his behalf, he states:

> Action inspired by confidence in the ultimate triumph of the Faith is, indeed, essential to the gradual and complete materialization of your hopes for the extension and consolidation of the Movement in your country.[43]

The Guardian also calls attention to the danger inherent in the friends' waiting until they are "<u>fully</u> qualified to do any particular task",[44] and he stresses the relationship between individual effort and divine assistance, observing that:

> God will … assist us if we do our share and sacrifice in the path of the progress of His Faith. We have to feel the responsibility laid upon our shoulders, arise to carry it out, and then expect divine grace to be showered upon us.[45]

3. Promoting Entry by Troops

From a study of the attached compilation, it is apparent that there are a number of specific activities that contribute directly to the process of entry by troops.

3.1 Strengthening of Spiritual Assemblies

Shoghi Effendi stresses the importance of the "instrumentality" of the Administrative Order in "vividly" and "systematically" bringing the healing Message of Bahá'u'lláh "to the attention of the masses".[46] He emphasizes the relationship between the development of the institutions and "the acceleration in the vital process of individual conversion", affirming that this latter is the reason for which "the entire machinery of the Administrative Order has been primarily and so laboriously erected".[47] Likewise, the Universal House of Justice directly links the strengthening and development of Local Spiritual Assemblies with the capacity of the Faith to deal with entry by troops.[48] The nature of this relationship is explained by the House of Justice in the 1993 Ridván message. It refers to "the mutuality of teaching and administration" and the fact that "each reinforces the other".[49]

The House of Justice indicates that there is an imperative need for Bahá'í institutions to

> improve their performance, through a closer identification with the fundamental verities of the Faith, through greater conformity to the spirit and form of Bahá'í administration and through a keener reliance on the beneficial effects of proper consultation, so that the communities they guide will

reflect a pattern of life that will offer hope to the disillusioned members of society.[50]

To this end, the Universal House of Justice stresses the importance of training the friends, including those in mass teaching areas,[51] to increase their understanding of and participation in the administrative work of the Cause. It notes that the "proper functioning" of the Spiritual Assemblies

> depends largely on the efforts of their members to familiarize themselves with their duties and to adhere scrupulously to principle in their personal behaviour and in the conduct of their official responsibilities.

It calls attention to the importance of the Assembly members'

> resolve to remove all traces of estrangement and sectarian tendencies from their midst, their ability to win the affection and support of the friends under their care and to involve as many individuals as possible in the work of the Cause.

And it affirms that the outcome of such dedicated effort on the part of the members of the institutions will result in "a pattern of life" that will not only be "a credit to the Faith" but will also serve to attract the "increasingly disillusioned members of society".[52]

3.2 Efficient Administration and Prompt Consolidation

While the way in which the teaching work is organized is a matter for each National Spiritual Assembly to determine, the Universal House of Justice stresses the need for "an efficient teaching structure" to ensure that "the tasks are carried out with dispatch and in accordance with the administrative principles of our Faith".[53] It further states that the work of consolidation, which is "an essential and inseparable element of teaching",[54] must be "prompt, thorough and continuing".[55] Such an integrated approach to the expansion of the Cause not only increases the human and financial resources of the Bahá'í community,[56] it also helps to avoid such problems as the inoculation" of believers against the Faith, resulting from a combination of inadequate teaching and careless consolidation.[57]

3.3 Strategic, Flexible Teaching Plans

The Universal House of Justice calls upon each National Spiritual Assembly to "balance its resources and harmonize its efforts" to ensure that the Faith is taught to "all sections of society".[58] It advises the Assemblies to be strategic and systematic, to tailor their teaching plans to meet the needs of particular social and cultural groups,[59] since "different cultures and types of people require different methods of approach",[60] and it states that the aim of all Bahá'í institutions and Bahá'í teachers is "to advance continually to new areas and strata of society".[61]

The House of Justice draws attention to the importance of flexibility and balance in the formulation and implementation of teaching plans. The believers are encouraged to be open to new methods,[62] to use a variety of approaches,[63] and "not blindly insist upon doing the same thing everywhere".[64] The Universal House of Justice indicates that the Bahá'í community

> must become more adept at accommodating a wide range of actions without losing concentration on the primary objectives of teaching, namely, expansion and consolidation.

And to this end, it stresses the need for

> a unity in diversity of actions ..., a condition in which different individuals will concentrate on different activities, appreciating the salutary effect of the aggregate on the growth and development of the Faith, because each person cannot do everything and all persons cannot do the same thing.[65]

The importance of the adoption by the believers of a strategic and flexible approach to the work of the Cause is linked by the Universal House of Justice both to the growing maturity of the Bahá'í community and to its expansion.[66]

3.4 Reaching People of Capacity

Writing to the National Spiritual Assemblies, the Universal House of Justice directed that the Faith must be carried "to every stratum of human society and every walk of life". It further stated that "all must be brought consciously within the teaching plans of the Bahá'í Community."[67]

Given the need to increase and develop the human resources of the Faith, the Universal House of Justice calls upon the believers to address special efforts to attracting people of capacity to the Cause.[68] It describes the enrolment of people of capacity as "an indispensable aspect of teaching the masses", and cautions that failure to achieve this end will result in the Faith's not being able "adequately to meet the challenges being thrust upon it". Concerning the membership of the Bahá'í community and the priorities for the teaching work, the House of Justice states:

> Its membership, regardless of ethnic variety, needs now to embrace increasing numbers of people of capacity, including persons of accomplishment and prominence in the various fields of human endeavour. Enrolling significant numbers of such persons is an indispensable aspect of teaching the masses, an aspect which cannot any longer be neglected and which must be consciously and deliberately incorporated into our teaching work, so as to broaden its base and accelerate the process of entry by troops.[69]

3.5 Relating the Faith to Contemporary Social and Humanitarian Issues

In the Riḍván 1988 message, the Universal House of Justice listed the individual believer's "constant endeavour" to relate the Teachings of the Faith to "current issues" as one of the measures which contribute to "success in teaching".[70] The House of Justice also notes that the "Order brought by Bahá'u'lláh is intended to guide the progress and resolve the problems of society", and that the Bahá'í community is "clearly in the vanguard of the constructive forces at work on the planet". It calls attention to the need to develop and perfect the Bahá'í administrative system as a means of demonstrating the efficacy of this system to minister to the crying needs of humanity, and to offer it as a viable alternative" to the defective crumbling old world order.[71]

3.6 Goal-Directed Behaviour

Individual believers, Local and National Spiritual Assemblies are called upon to collaborate and persist in their efforts to achieve the goals of the teaching plans. The Universal House of Justice states:

> The teaching work, both that organized by institutions of the Faith and that which is the fruit of individual initiative, must be actively carried forward so that there will be growing numbers of believers, leading more countries to the stage of entry by troops and ultimately to mass conversion.[72]

The urgency of this undertaking is emphasized by the House of Justice, as follows:

> A massive expansion of the Bahá'í community must be achieved far beyond all past records. The task of spreading the Message to the generality of mankind in villages, towns and cities must be rapidly extended. The need for this is critical...[73]

In addition, the Universal House of Justice calls attention to the quality of the teaching enterprise, advising that "the effort of the Bahá'ís should be to teach not only as intensively as possible but also as well as possible".[74]

The ultimate responsibility of the individual believer for the implementation of the teaching work is underlined by the House of Justice. It states:

> Every individual believer—man, woman, youth and child —is summoned to this field of action; for it is on the initiative, the resolute will of the individual to teach and to serve, that the success of the entire community depends.[75]

And it affirms that:

> The key to the conversion of people to the Faith is the action of the individual Bahá'í conveying the spark of faith to individual seekers, answering their questions and deepening their understanding of the teachings.[76]

4. Concluding Remarks

The extracts contained in the compilation "Promoting Entry by Troops" serve to highlight a number of general principles relating to the nature of growth and its acceleration and to the attraction of large numbers of people to the Bahá'í Faith. In addition, the extracts suggest specific activities that can be undertaken, by individuals and institutions, to increase the tempo of growth and to sustain large-scale expansion of the Cause.

It is evident that forces without and within the Cause are shaping the destiny of humanity. The Universal House of Justice calls attention to the operation of two great processes that are at work in the world. The first process is

> the great Plan of God, tumultuous in its progress, working through mankind as a whole, tearing down barriers to world unity and forging humankind into a unified body in the fires of suffering and experience. This process will produce, in God's due time, the Lesser Peace, the political unification of the world. Mankind at that time can be likened to a body that is unified but without life. The second process, the task of breathing life into this unified body—of creating true unity and spirituality culminating in the Most Great Peace—is that of the Bahá'ís, who are labouring consciously, with detailed instructions and continuing divine guidance, to erect the fabric of the Kingdom of God on earth, into which they call their fellow-men, thus conferring upon them eternal life.[77]

The challenge to the believers is to devote all their energies to this vital task, spurred on by the realization that "there is no one else to do it",[78] and sustained by their desire to fulfil the longing expressed by the beloved Guardian in the earliest days of his ministry:

> And now as I look into the future, I hope to see the friends at all times, in every land, and of every shade of thought and character, voluntarily and joyously rallying round their local and in particular their national centres of activity, upholding and promoting their interests with complete unanimity and contentment, with perfect understanding, genuine

enthusiasm, and sustained vigour. This indeed is the one joy and yearning of my life, for it is the fountain-head from which all future blessings will flow, the broad foundation upon which the security of the Divine Edifice must ultimately rest. May we not hope that now at last the dawn of a brighter day is breaking upon our beloved Cause?[79]

REFERENCES

Note: The numbers in brackets following each reference correspond
to the numbering of the extracts in the attached compilation.

1. Letter dated 25 June 1953 written by Shoghi Effendi, published
in "Citadel of Faith: Messages to America 1947-1957"
(Wilmette: Bahá'í Publishing Trust, 1980), p. 117 **[18]***

2. Riḍván 1990 message written by the Universal House of Justice
to the Bahá'ís of the world **[45]**

3. See extract **[2]**

4. See extract **[33]**

5. Letter dated 31 August 1987 written by the Universal House of
Justice to the Bahá'ís of the world **[39]**

6. Letter dated 30 June 1952 written on behalf of Shoghi Effendi
to a National Spiritual Assembly **[17]**

7. Naw-Rúz 1979 message written by the Universal House of
Justice to the Bahá'ís of the world **[32]**; see also extracts **[34]**
and **[44]**

8. See extract **[41]**

9. Letter dated 12 September 1991 written on behalf of the
Universal House of Justice to a National Spiritual Assembly **[46]**

10. Riḍván 1987 message written by the Universal House of Justice
to the Bahá'ís of the world **[38]**

11. See extract **[44]**

12. See extract **[21]**

13. Postcript in the handwriting of Shoghi Effendi appended to a
letter dated 12 August 1941 written on his behalf, cf. "Messages
to America: Selected Letters and Cablegrams Addressed to the
Bahá'ís of North America, 1932-1946" (Wilmette: Bahá'í
Publishing Committee, 1947), p. 51 **[6]**

---

* Published version gives date as 18 July 1953.

14.   See extract **[40]**

15.   Message dated 27 December 1985 written by the Universal House of Justice to the Conference of the Continental Boards of Counsellors **[36]**

16.   See extracts **[4]** and **[13]**

17.   Letter dated 5 October 1953 written on behalf of Shoghi Effendi to an individual believer **[19]**

18.   See extract **[24]**

19.   See extract **[38]**

20.   Ridván 1988 message written by the Universal House of Justice to the Bahá'ís of the world **[40]**

21.   Ridván 1993 message written by the Universal House of Justice to the Bahá'ís of the world **[48]**

22.   Ridván 1988 message written by the Universal House of Justice to the Bahá'ís of the world **[40]**

23.   See extracts **[35]**, **[44]**, and **[47]**

24.   Letter dated 18 February 1932 written on behalf of Shoghi Effendi to an individual believer **[2]**

25.   Ridván 1989 message written by the Universal House of Justice to the Bahá'ís of the world **[44]**

26.   See extracts **[16]** and **[40]**

27.   See extract **[25]**

28.   Letter dated 19 March 1954 written on behalf of Shoghi Effendi to a Local Spiritual Assembly **[20]**

29.   See extract **[8]**

30.   See extract **[15]**

31.   Letter dated 13 March 1944 written on behalf of Shoghi Effendi to a Bahá'í winter school session **[9]**; see also extract **[11]**

32.   Letter dated 25 March 1949 written on behalf of Shoghi Effendi to an individual believer **[14]**

33.   Letter dated 30 June 1993 written on behalf of the Universal House of Justice to an individual believer **[49]**

34. Ridván 1993 message written by the Universal House of Justice to the Bahá'ís of the world **[48]**

35. See extract **[40]**

36. Letter dated 13 July 1964 written by the Universal House of Justice to all National Spiritual Assemblies, cf. "Wellspring of Guidance: Messages 1963-1968" (Wilmette: Bahá'í Publishing Trust, 1976), pp. 31-33 **[23]**

37. Letter dated 2 February 1966 written by the Universal House of Justice to all National Spiritual Assemblies engaged in mass teaching work **[25]**

38. Ridván 1990 message written by the Universal House of Justice to the Bahá'ís of the world **[45]**

39. Letter dated 17 April 1981 written by the Universal House of Justice to all National Spiritual Assemblies **[35]**

40. Letter dated 13 March 1944 written on behalf of Shoghi Effendi to an individual believer **[10]**

41. Message dated August 1968 written by the Universal House of Justice to the Palermo Conference, cf. "Messages from the Universal House of Justice, 1968-1973" (Wilmette: Bahá'í Publishing Trust, 1976), p. 12 **[28]**

42. Ridván 1990 message written by the Universal House of Justice to the Bahá'ís of the world **[45]**

43. Letter dated 11 May 1934 written on behalf of Shoghi Effendi to an individual believer **[5]**

44. Letter dated 4 May 1942 written on behalf of Shoghi Effendi to an individual believer **[7]**

45. Letter dated 20 December 1932 written on behalf of Shoghi Effendi to a National Spiritual Assembly **[3]**

46. Postcript in the handwriting of Shoghi Effendi appended to a letter dated 29 March 1945 written on his behalf to a National Spiritual Assembly **[12]**

47. Postcript in the handwriting of Shoghi Effendi appended to a letter dated 12 August 1957 written on his behalf to a National Spiritual Assembly **[22]**

48. See extract [30]

49. Riḍván 1993 message written by the Universal House of Justice to the Bahá'ís of the world [48]

50. Riḍván 1990 message written by the Universal House of Justice to the Bahá'ís of the world [45]

51. See extract [32]

52. Riḍván 1993 message written by the Universal House of Justice to the Bahá'ís of the world [48]

53. Letter dated 2 February 1966 written by the Universal House of Justice to all National Spiritual Assemblies engaged in mass teaching work [25]

54. Letter dated 16 April 1981 written on behalf of the Universal House of Justice to all Continental Pioneer Committees [34]

55. Naw-Rúz 1979 message written by the Universal House of Justice to the Bahá'ís of the world [32]

56. See extract [36]

57. See extract [34]

58. Letter dated 13 July 1964 written by the Universal House of Justice to all National Spiritual Assemblies, cf. "Wellspring of Guidance", pp. 31-33 [23]

59. See extract [26]

60. Letter dated 11 August 1988 written on behalf of the Universal House of Justice to an individual believer [41]

61. Letter dated 25 May 1975 written by the Universal House of Justice to all National Spiritual Assemblies [31]

62. See extract [29]

63. See extract [43]

64. Letter dated 13 November 1986 written on behalf of the Universal House of Justice to a National Spiritual Assembly [37]

65. Riḍván 1990 message written by the Universal House of Justice to the Bahá'ís of the world [45]

66. See extract [37]

67.   Letter dated 31 October 1967 written by the Universal House of Justice to all National Spiritual Assemblies, cf. "Wellspring of Guidance", pp. 124-25 **[26]**

68.   See extract **[48]**

69.   Riḍván 1990 message written by the Universal House of Justice to the Bahá'ís of the world **[45]**

70.   Riḍván 1988 message written by the Universal House of Justice to the Bahá'ís of the world **[40]**

71.   Riḍván 1990 message written by the Universal House of Justice to the Bahá'ís of the world **[45]**

72.   Naw-Rúz 1979 message written by the Universal House of Justice to the Bahá'ís of the world **[32]**

73.   Riḍván 1993 message written by the Universal House of Justice to the Bahá'ís of the world **[48]**

74.   Letter dated 1 November 1988 written on behalf of the Universal House of Justice to a National Spiritual Assembly **[42]**

75.   Riḍván 1988 message written by the Universal House of Justice to the Bahá'ís of the world **[40]**

76.   Letter dated 9 February 1989 written on behalf of the Universal House of Justice to a National Spiritual Assembly **[43]**

77.   Letter dated 8 December 1967 written by the Universal House of Justice to an individual believer, cf. "Wellspring of Guidance", pp. 133-34 **[27]**

78.   ibid., p. 134 **[27]**

79.   Letter dated 24 September 1924 written by Shoghi Effendi to the Bahá'ís of America, published in "Bahá'í Administration: Selected Messages 1922-1932" (Wilmette: Bahá'í Publishing Trust, 1974), p. 67 **[1]**

PROMOTING ENTRY BY TROOPS

A Compilation of Extracts from Letters Written by or on Behalf
of Shoghi Effendi and the Universal House of Justice
Prepared by the Research Department
October 1993

From Letters Written by or on Behalf of Shoghi Effendi

1.   And now as I look into the future, I hope to see the friends at all
times, in every land, and of every shade of thought and character,
voluntarily and joyously rallying round their local and in particular
their national centres of activity, upholding and promoting their
interests with complete unanimity and contentment, with perfect
understanding, genuine enthusiasm, and sustained vigour. This
indeed is the one joy and yearning of my life, for it is the fountain-head
from which all future blessings will flow, the broad foundation upon
which the security of the Divine Edifice must ultimately rest. May we
not hope that now at last the dawn of a brighter day is breaking upon
our beloved Cause?
(24 September 1924, written by Shoghi Effendi to the Bahá'ís of America,
published in "Bahá'í Administration: Selected Messages 1922-1932"
(Wilmette: Bahá'í Publishing Trust, 1974), p. 67)

2.   The work that the members of your small family are doing in
spreading the Cause and infusing its divine spirit among the people
you meet, is a fact that no one familiar with your life can deny.... In
time you will see how abundant the fruit of your services will be. It is
not sufficient to number the souls that embrace the Cause to know
the progress that it is making. The more important consequences of
your activities are the spirit that is diffused into the life of the
community, and the extent to which the teachings we proclaim
become part of the consciousness and belief of the people that hear
them. For it is only when the spirit has thoroughly permeated the
world that the people will begin to enter the Faith in large numbers.
At the beginning of spring only the few, exceptionally favoured seeds

will sprout, but when the season gets in its full sway, and the atmosphere gets permeated with the warmth of true springtime, then masses of flowers will begin to appear, and a whole hillside suddenly blooms. We are still in the state when only isolated souls are awakened, but soon we shall have the full swing of the season and the quickening of whole groups and nations into the spiritual life breathed by Bahá'u'lláh.

(18 February 1932, written on behalf of Shoghi Effendi to an individual believer)

3. ...with God's help, he trusts, you will succeed. He will surely reinforce your efforts and assist you in the completion of that task that lies before you. God will, however, assist us if we do our share and sacrifice in the path of the progress of His Faith. We have to feel the responsibility laid upon our shoulders, arise to carry it out, and then expect divine grace to be showered upon us.

(20 December 1932, written on behalf of Shoghi Effendi to a National Spiritual Assembly)

4. Must humanity, tormented as she now is, be afflicted with still severer tribulations ere their purifying influence can prepare her to enter the heavenly Kingdom destined to be established upon earth? Must the inauguration of so vast, so unique, so illumined an era in human history be ushered in by so great a catastrophe in human affairs as to recall, nay surpass, the appalling collapse of Roman civilization in the first centuries of the Christian era? Must a series of profound convulsions stir and rock the human race ere Bahá'u'lláh can be enthroned in the hearts and consciences of the masses, ere His undisputed ascendency is universally recognized, and the noble edifice of His World Order is reared and established?

(11 March 1936, written by Shoghi Effendi, published in "The World Order of Bahá'u'lláh: Selected Letters" (Wilmette: Bahá'í Publishing Trust, 1991), pp. 201-2)

5. Action inspired by confidence in the ultimate triumph of the Faith is, indeed, essential to the gradual and complete materialization of your hopes for the extension and consolidation of the Movement in your

25.   It has been due to the splendid victories in large-scale conversion that the Faith of Bahá'u'lláh has entered a new phase in its development and establishment throughout the world. It is imperative, therefore, that the process of teaching the masses be not only maintained but accelerated. The teaching committee structure that each National Assembly may adopt to ensure best results in the extension of its teaching work is a matter left entirely to its discretion, but an efficient teaching structure there must be, so that the tasks are carried out with dispatch and in accordance with the administrative principles of our Faith. From among the believers native to each country, competent travelling teachers must be selected and teaching projects worked out....

While this vital teaching work is progressing each National Assembly must ever bear in mind that expansion and consolidation are inseparable processes that must go hand in hand.... To ensure that the spiritual life of the individual believer is continuously enriched, that local communities are becoming increasingly conscious of their collective duties, and that the institutions of an evolving administration are operating efficiently, is, therefore, as important as expanding into new fields and bringing in the multitudes under the shadow of the Cause.

(2 February 1966, written by the Universal House of Justice to all National Spiritual Assemblies engaged in mass teaching work)

26.   The paramount goal of the teaching work at the present time is to carry the message of Bahá'u'lláh to every stratum of human society and every walk of life. An eager response to the teachings will often be found in the most unexpected quarters, and any such response should be quickly followed up, for success in a fertile area awakens a response in those who were at first uninterested.

The same presentation of the teachings will not appeal to everybody; the method of expression and the approach must be varied in accordance with the outlook and interests of the hearer. An approach which is designed to appeal to everybody will usually result in attracting the middle section, leaving both extremes untouched. No effort must be spared to ensure that the healing Word of God reaches the rich and the poor, the learned and the illiterate, the old and the young, the devout and the atheist, the dweller in the remote hills and islands, the inhabitants of the teeming cities, the suburban businessman, the labourer in the slums, the nomadic tribesman, the farmer, the university student; all must be brought consciously within the teaching plans of the Bahá'í Community.

Whereas plans must be carefully made, and every useful means adopted in the furtherance of this work, your Assemblies must never let such plans eclipse the shining truth expounded in the enclosed quotations: that it is the purity of heart, detachment, uprightness, devotion and love of the teacher that attracts the divine confirmations and enables him, however ignorant he be in this world's learning, to win the hearts of his fellowmen to the Cause of God.

(31 October 1967, written by the Universal House of Justice to all National Spiritual Assemblues, cf. "Wellspring of Guidance", pp. 124-25)

27.   We are told by Shoghi Effendi that two great processes are at work in the world: the great Plan of God, tumultuous in its progress, working through mankind as a whole, tearing down barriers to world unity and forging humankind into a unified body in the fires of suffering and experience. This process will produce, in God's due time, the Lesser Peace, the political unification of the world. Mankind at that time can be likened to a body that is unified but without life. The second process, the task of breathing life into this unified body — of creating true unity and spirituality culminating in the Most Great Peace — is that of the Bahá'ís, who are labouring consciously, with detailed instructions and continuing divine guidance, to erect the fabric of the Kingdom of God on earth, into which they call their fellow-men, thus conferring upon them eternal life.

The working out of God's Major Plan proceeds mysteriously in ways directed by Him alone, but the Minor Plan that He has given us to execute, as our part in His grand design for the redemption of mankind, is clearly delineated. It is to this work that we must devote all our energies, for there is no one else to do it.

(8 December 1967, written by the Universal House of Justice to an individual believer, cf. "Wellspring of Guidance", pp. 133-34)

28. Wherever a Bahá'í community exists, whether large or small, let it be distinguished for its abiding sense of security and faith, its high standard of rectitude, its complete freedom from all forms of prejudice, the spirit of love among its members and for the closely knit fabric of its social life. The acute distinction between this and present-day society will inevitably arouse the interest of the more enlightened, and as the world's gloom deepens the light of Bahá'í life will shine even brighter and brighter until its brilliance must eventually attract the disillusioned masses and cause them to enter the haven of the Covenant of Bahá'u'lláh, Who alone can bring them peace and justice and an ordered life.

(August 1968, message written by the Universal House of Justice to the Palermo Conference, cf. "Messages from the Universal House of Justice, 1968-1973" (Wilmette: Bahá'í Publishing Trust, 1976), p. 12)

29. We note that the new teaching methods you have developed, in reaching the waiting masses, have substantially influenced the winning of your goals, and we urge the American Bahá'ís, one and all, newly enrolled and believers of long standing, to arise, put their reliance in Bahá'u'lláh and armed with that supreme power, continue unabated their efforts to reach the waiting souls, while simultaneously consolidating the hard-won victories. New methods inevitably bring with them criticism and challenges no matter how successful they may ultimately prove to be. The influx of so many new believers is, in itself, a call to the veteran believers to join the ranks of those in this field of service and to give wholeheartedly of their knowledge and experience. Far from standing aloof, the American believers are called upon now, as never before, to grasp this golden opportunity which has been presented to them, to consult together prayerfully and widen the scope of their endeavours.

Efforts to reach the minorities should be increased and broadened to include all minority groups such as the Indians, Spanish-speaking people, Japanese and Chinese. Indeed, every stratum of American society must be reached and can be reached with the healing Message, if the believers will but arise and go forth with the spirit which is conquering the citadels of the southern states. Such a programme, coupled as it must be with continuous consolidation, can be effectively carried out by universal participation on the part of every lover of Bahá'u'lláh.

(14 February 1972, written by the Universal House of Justice to the National Spiritual Assembly of the United States, published in "Messages from the Universal House of Justice, 1968-1973", pp. 85-86)

30.   Strengthening and development of Local Spiritual Assemblies is a vital objective of the Five Year Plan. Success in this one goal will greatly enrich the quality of Bahá'í life, will heighten the capacity of the Faith to deal with entry by troops which is even now taking place and, above all, will demonstrate the solidarity and ever-growing distinctiveness of the Bahá'í community, thereby attracting more and more thoughtful souls to the Faith and offering a refuge to the leaderless and hapless millions of the spiritually bankrupt, moribund present order.

(Naw-Rúz 1974 message written by the Universal House of Justice to the Bahá'ís of the world)

31.   Teaching the Faith embraces many diverse activities, all of which are vital to success, and each of which reinforces the other....

The aim, therefore, of all Bahá'í institutions and Bahá'í teachers is to advance continually to new areas and strata of society, with such thoroughness that, as the spark of faith kindles the hearts of the hearers, the teaching of the believers continues until, and even after, they shoulder their responsibilities as Bahá'ís and participate in both the teaching and administrative work of the Faith.

There are now many areas in the world where thousands of people have accepted the Faith so quickly that it has been beyond the capacity of the existing communities to consolidate adequately these advances. The people in these areas must be progressively deepened in their understanding of the Faith, in accordance with well-laid plans, so that their communities may, as soon as possible, become sources of great strength to the work of the Faith and begin to manifest the pattern of Bahá'í life.

(25 May 1975, written by the Universal House of Justice to all National Spiritual Assemblies)

32.   In many lands, however, there is an eager receptivity for the teachings of the Faith. The challenge for the Bahá'ís is to provide these thousands of seeking souls, as swiftly as possible, with the spiritual food that they crave, to enlist them under the banner of Bahá'u'lláh, to nurture them in the way of life He has revealed, and to guide them to elect Local Spiritual Assemblies which, as they begin to function strongly, will unite the friends in firmly consolidated Bahá'í communities and become beacons of guidance and havens of refuge to mankind....

Throughout the world the Seven Year Plan must witness the attainment of the following objectives:...

  – The teaching work, both that organized by institutions of the Faith and that which is the fruit of individual initiative, must be actively carried forward so that there will be growing numbers of believers, leading more countries to the stage of entry by troops and ultimately to mass conversion.

  – This teaching work must include prompt, thorough and continuing consolidation so that all victories will be safeguarded, the number of Local Spiritual Assemblies will be increased and the foundations of the Cause reinforced.

(Naw-Rúz 1979 message written by the Universal House of Justice to the Bahá'ís of the world)

33.   The Faith of God does not advance at one uniform pace. Sometimes it is like the advance of the sea when the tide is rising. Meeting a sandbank the water seems to be held back, but, with a new wave, it surges forward, flooding past the barrier which checked it for a little while. If the friends will but persist in their efforts, the cumulative effect of years of work will suddenly appear.

(27 July 1980, written by the Universal House of Justice to a National Spiritual Assembly)

34.   The ... problem occurs most frequently in countries such as those in Africa, where there is entry by troops. In such countries it is comparatively easy to bring large numbers of new believers into the Faith, and this is such a thrilling experience that visiting teachers often tend to prefer to do this rather than help with the consolidation work.... It should be pointed out that, especially if they [the travelling teachers] are assigned to expansion work, they must remember that consolidation is an essential and inseparable element of teaching, and if they go to a remote area and enrol believers whom no one is going to be able to visit again in the near future, they may well be doing a disservice to those people and to the Faith. To give people this glorious Message and then to leave them in the lurch, produces disappointment and disillusionment, so that, when it does become possible to carry out properly planned teaching in that area, the teachers may well find the people resistant to the Message. The first teacher who was careless of consolidation, instead of planting and nourishing the seeds of faith has, in fact, "inoculated" the people against the Divine Message and made subsequent teaching very much harder.

(16 April 1981, written on behalf of the Universal House of Justice to all Continental Pioneer Committees)

35.   Consolidation is as vital a part of the teaching work as expansion. It is that aspect of teaching which assists the believers to deepen their knowledge and understanding of the Teachings, and fans the flame of their devotion to Bahá'u'lláh and His Cause, so that they will, of their own volition, continue the process of their spiritual development, promote the teaching work, and strengthen the functioning of their administrative institutions. Proper consolidation is essential to the preservation of the spiritual health of the community, to the protection of its interests, to the upholding of its good name, and ultimately to the continuation of the work of expansion itself.

(17 April 1981, written on behalf of the Universal House of Justice to all National Spiritual Assemblies)

36.   Who can doubt that we are now entering a period of unprecedented and unimaginable developments in the onward march of the Faith?... We know that the present victories will lead to active opposition, for which the Bahá'í world community must be prepared. We know the prime needs of the Cause at the moment: a vast expansion of its numbers and financial resources; a greater consolidation of its community life and the authority of its institutions; an observable increase in those characteristics of loving unity, stability of family life, freedom from prejudice and rectitude of conduct which must distinguish the Bahá'ís from the spiritually lost and wayward multitudes around them. Surely the time cannot be long delayed when we must deal universally with that entry by troops foretold by the Master as a prelude to mass conversion.

(27 December 1985, message written by the Universal House of Justice to the Conference of the Continental Boards of Counsellors)

7.   The House of Justice read with much interest the circumstances which inspired the new impetus being experienced in your teaching activities and was happy to learn that the ... believers are themselves taking a more active part in the teaching work. This trend should by all means be encouraged by your Assembly, which should do everything in its power to ensure that increasing numbers of native believers are deepened in the verities of the Faith and encouraged to teach not only through the means recently opened to them, but through the variety of approaches which are possible in different parts of the country and among different strata of ... society. While taking the fullest advantage of a workable method in one area, the friends should be open to other methods and not blindly insist upon doing the same thing everywhere. If such flexibility is understood, your community will surely grow in numbers and strength.

(13 November 1986, written on behalf of the Universal House of Justice to a National Spiritual Assembly)

38.   The stage is set for universal, rapid and massive growth of the Cause of God.... The all-important teaching work must be imaginatively, persistently and sacrificially continued, ensuring the enrolment of ever larger numbers who will provide the energy, the resources and spiritual force to enable the beloved Cause to worthily play its part in the redemption of mankind.

(Riḍván 1987 message written by the Universal House of Justice to the Bahá'ís of the world)

39. The Faith advances, not at a uniform rate of growth, but in vast surges, precipitated by the alternation of crisis and victory. In a passage written on 18 July 1953, in the early months of the Ten Year Crusade, Shoghi Effendi, referring to the vital need to ensure through the teaching work a "steady flow" of "fresh recruits to the slowly yet steadily advancing army of the Lord of Hosts", stated that this flow would "presage and hasten the advent of the day which, as prophesied by 'Abdu'l-Bahá, will witness the entry by troops of peoples of divers nations and races into the Bahá'í world". This day the Bahá'í world has already seen in Africa, the Pacific, in Asia and in Latin America, and this process of entry by troops must, in the present plan, be augmented and spread to other countries for, as the Guardian stated in this same letter, it "will be the prelude to that long-awaited hour when a mass conversion on the part of these same nations and races, and as a direct result of a chain of events, momentous and possibly catastrophic in nature, and which cannot as yet be even dimly visualized, will suddenly revolutionize the fortunes of the Faith, derange the equilibrium of the world, and reinforce a thousandfold the numerical strength as well as the material power and the spiritual authority of the Faith of Bahá'u'lláh". This is the time for which we must now prepare ourselves; this is the hour whose coming it is our task to hasten.

(31 August 1987, written by the Universal House of Justice to the Bahá'ís of the world)

40. A silver lining to the dark picture which has overshadowed most of this century now brightens the horizon. It is discernible in the new tendencies impelling the social processes at work throughout the world, in the evidences of an accelerated trend towards peace. In the Faith of God, it is the growing strength of the Order of Bahá'u'lláh as its banner rises to more stately heights. It is a strength that attracts. The media are giving increasing attention to the Bahá'í world community; authors are acknowledging its existence in a growing number of articles, books and reference works, one of the most highly respected of which recently listed the Faith as the most widely spread religion after Christianity. A remarkable display of interest in this community by governments, civil authorities, prominent personalities

and humanitarian organizations is increasingly apparent. Not only are the community's laws and principles, organization and way of life being investigated, but its advice and active help are also being sought for the alleviation of social problems and the carrying out of humanitarian activities.

A thrilling consequence of these favourably conjoined developments is the emergence of a new paradigm of opportunity for further growth and consolidation of our world-wide community. New prospects for teaching the Cause at all levels of society have unfolded. These are confirmed in the early results flowing from the new teaching initiatives being fostered in a number of places as more and more national communities witness the beginnings of that entry by troops promised by the beloved Master and which Shoghi Effendi said would lead on to mass conversion. The immediate possibilities presented by this providential situation compel us to expect that an expansion of the Community of the Most Great Name, such as has not yet been experienced, is, indeed, at hand.

The spark which ignited the mounting interest in the Cause of Bahá'u'lláh was the heroic fortitude and patience of the beloved friends in Irán, which moved the Bahá'í world community to conduct a persistent, carefully orchestrated programme of appeal to the conscience of the world. This vast undertaking, involving the entire community acting unitedly through its Administrative Order, was accompanied by equally vigorous and visible activities of that community in other spheres which have been detailed separately. Nonetheless, we are impelled to mention that an important outcome of this extensive exertion is our recognition of a new stage in the external affairs of the Cause, characterized by a marked maturation of National Spiritual Assemblies in their growing relations with governmental and non-governmental organizations and with the public in general....

But the paramount purpose of all Bahá'í activity is teaching. All that has been done or will be done revolves around this central activity, the "head corner-stone of the foundation itself", to which all progress in the Cause is due. The present challenge calls for teaching on a scale and of a quality, a variety, and intensity outstripping all current efforts. The time is now, lest opportunity be lost in the swiftly changing moods of a frenetic world. Let it not be imagined that expedience is the essential motive arousing this sense of urgency. There is an overarching reason: it is the pitiful plight of masses of humanity, suffering and in turmoil, hungering after righteousness, but "bereft of discernment to see God with there own eyes, or hear His Melody with their own ears". They must be fed. Vision must be restored where hope is lost, confidence built where doubt and confusion are rife. In these and other respects, "The Promise of World Peace" is designed to open the way. Its delivery to national governmental leaders having been virtually completed, its contents must now be conveyed, by all possible means, to peoples everywhere from all walks of life. This is a necessary part of the teaching work in our time and must be pursued with unabated vigour.

Teaching is the food of the spirit; it brings life to unawakened souls and raises the new heaven and the new earth; it uplifts the banner of a unified world; it ensures the victory of the Covenant and brings those who give their lives to it the supernal happiness of attainment to the good pleasure of their Lord.

Every individual believer — man, woman, youth and child — is summoned to this field of action; for it is on the initiative, the resolute will of the individual to teach and to serve, that the success of the entire community depends. Well-grounded in the mighty Covenant of Bahá'u'lláh, sustained by daily prayer and reading of the Holy Word, strengthened by a continual striving to obtain a deeper understanding of the divine Teachings, illumined by a constant endeavour to relate these Teachings to current issues, nourished by observance of the laws and principles of His wondrous World Order, every individual can attain increasing measures of success in teaching. In sum, the ultimate triumph of the Cause is assured by that "one thing and only one thing" so poignantly emphasized by Shoghi Effendi, namely, "the extent to which our own inner life and private character mirror forth in their manifold aspects the spendour of those eternal principles proclaimed by Bahá'u'lláh".

(Riḍván 1988 message written by the Universal House of Justice to the Bahá'ís of the world)

41.   Your concern about consolidation and "mass teaching" is noted. The concept of mass teaching may be better understood if put in the context of "teaching the masses". This implies reaching every level of society in every continent and island in the world. In developing countries large segments of the population have become Bahá'ís, usually among the less educated. More recently, particularly in Asia, we see that the youth in high schools and colleges have been attracted to the Faith in large numbers. This does not mean, however, that there is any particular system of teaching which individual Bahá'ís should pursue. Different cultures and types of people require different methods of approach. While taking the fullest advantage of a workable method in one area, the friends should be open to other methods and not blindly insist upon doing the same thing everywhere. If such flexibility is understood, the ... community will surely grow in numbers and strength.

(11 August 1988, written on behalf of the Universal House of Justice to an individual believer)

42. What is required is a sense of urgency in **teaching** and this means to ignite the spark of faith and devotion in the hearts of the people and fan it so that those who accept the Faith become its firm and ardent supporters. Inevitably some of those who are attracted to the Message and declare their acceptance of it will later drift away from the Cause — this is in the nature of the human response to all teachings — but the effort of the Bahá'ís should be to teach not only as intensively as possible but also as well as possible.

(1 November 1988, written on behalf of the Universal House of Justice to a National Spiritual Assembly)

43.   The International Teaching Centre has concluded that the Bahá'í institutions in ... seem to have been placing too much reliance on large, expensive projects, involving a great deal of successful public relations and proclamation. These are, in their own way, very useful activities, but it must be realized that they cannot be expected to produce large numbers of new believers. The key to the conversion of people to the Faith is the action of the individual Bahá'í conveying the spark of faith to individual seekers, answering their questions and deepening their understanding of the teachings.

(9 February 1989, written on behalf of the Universal House of Justice to a National Spiritual Assembly)

44.   The spiritual current which exerted such galvanic effects at the International Bahá'í Convention last Riḍván has swept through the entire world community, arousing its members in both the East and the West to feats of activity and achievement in teaching never before experienced in any one year. The high level of enrolments alone bears this out, as nearly half a million new believers have already been reported. The names of such far-flung places as India and Liberia, Bolivia and Bangladesh, Taiwan and Peru, the Philippines and Haiti leap to the fore as we contemplate the accumulating evidences of the entry by troops called for in our message of a year ago. These are hopeful signs of the greater acceleration yet to come and in which all national communities, whatever the current status of their teaching effort, will ultimately be involved....

All these requirements must and will surely be met through reconsecrated service on the part of every conscientous member of the Community of Bahá, and particularly through personal commitment to the teaching work. So fundamentally important is this work to ensuring the foundation for success in all Bahá'í undertakings and to furthering the process of entry by troops that we are moved to add a word of emphasis for your consideration. It is not enough to proclaim the Bahá'í message, essential as that is. It is not enough to expand the rolls of Bahá'í membership, vital as that is. Souls must be transformed, communities thereby consolidated, new models of life thus attained. Transformation is the essential purpose of the Cause of Bahá'u'lláh, but it lies in the will and effort of the individual to achieve it in obedience to the Covenant. Necessary to the progress of this life-fulfilling transformation is knowledge of the will and purpose of God through regular reading and study of the Holy Word.

Beloved Friends: The momentum generated by this past year's achievements is reflected not only in the opportunities for marked expansion of the Cause but also in a broad range of challenges — momentous, insistent and varied — which have combined in ways that place demands beyond any previous measure upon our spiritual and material resources. We must be prepared to meet them. At this mid-point of the Six Year Plan, we have reached a historic moment pregnant with hopes and possibilities — a moment at which significant trends in the world are becoming more closely aligned with principles and objectives of the Cause of God. The urgency upon our community to press onward in fulfilment of its world-embracing mission is therefore tremendous.

Our primary response must be to teach — teach ourselves and to teach others — at all levels of society, by all possible means, and without further delay.

(Riḍván 1989 message written by the Universal House of Justice to the
Bahá'ís of the world)

45. Over the last two years, almost one million souls entered the Cause. The increasing instances of entry by troops in different places contributed to that growth, drawing attention to Shoghi Effendi's vision which shapes our perception of glorious future possibilities in the teaching field. For he has asserted that the process of "entry by troops of peoples of divers nations and races into the Bahá'í world ... will be the prelude to that long-awaited hour when a mass conversion on the part of these same nations and races, and as a direct result of a chain of events, momentous and possibly catastrophic in nature, and which cannot as yet be even dimly visualized, will suddenly revolutionize the fortunes of the Faith, derange the equilibrium of the world, and reinforce a thousandfold the numerical strength as well as the material power and the spiritual authority of the Faith of Bahá'u'lláh". We have every encouragement to believe that large-scale enrolments will expand, involving village after village, town after town, from one country to another. However, it is not for us to wait passively for the ultimate fulfilment of Shoghi Effendi's vision. We few, placing our whole trust in the providence of God and regarding as a divine privilege the challenges which face us, must proceed to victory with the plans in hand.

An expansion of thought and action in certain aspects of our work would enhance our possibilities for success in meeting our aforementioned commitments. Since change, ever more rapid change, is a constant characteristic of life at this time, and since our growth, size and external relations demand much of us, our community must be ready to adapt. In a sense this means that the community must become more adept at accommodating a wide range of actions without losing concentration on the primary objectives of teaching, namely, expansion and consolidation. A unity in diversity of actions is called for, a condition in which different individuals will concentrate on different activities, appreciating the salutary effect of the aggregate on the growth and development of the Faith, because each person cannot do everything and all persons cannot do the same thing. This understanding is important to the maturity which, by the many demands being made upon it, the community is being forced to attain.

The Order brought by Bahá'u'lláh is intended to guide the progress and resolve the problems of society. Our numbers are as yet too small to effect an adequate demonstration of the potentialities inherent in the administrative system we are building, and the efficacy of this system will not be fully appreciated without a vast expansion of our membership. With the prevailing situation in the world the necessity to effect such a demonstration becomes more compelling. It is all too obvious that even those who rail against the defects of the old order, and would even tear it down, are themselves bereft of any viable alternative to put in its place. Since the Administrative Order is designed to be a pattern for future society, the visibility of such a pattern will be a signal of hope to those who despair.

Thus far, we have achieved a marvellous diversity in the large numbers of ethnic groups represented in the Faith, and everything should be done to fortify it through larger enrolments from among groups already represented and the attraction of members from groups not yet reached. However, there is another category of diversity which must be built up and without which the Cause will not be able adequately to meet the challenges being thrust upon it. Its membership, regardless of ethnic variety, needs now to embrace increasing numbers of people of capacity, including persons of accomplishment and prominence in the various fields of human endeavour. Enrolling significant numbers of such persons is an indispensible aspect of teaching the masses, an aspect which cannot any longer be neglected and which must be consciously and deliberately incorporated into our teaching work, so as to broaden its base and accelerate the process of entry by troops. So important and timely is the need for action on this matter that we are impelled to call upon Continental Counsellors and National Spiritual Assemblies to devote serious attention to it in their consultations and plans.

The affairs of mankind have reached a stage at which increasing calls will be made upon our community to assist, through advice and practical measures, in solving critical social problems. It is a service that we will gladly render, but this means that our Local and National Spiritual Assemblies must adhere more scrupulously to principle. With increasing public attention being focused on the Cause of God, it becomes imperative for Bahá'í institutions to improve their performance, through a closer identification with the fundamental verities of the Faith, through greater conformity to the spirit and form of Bahá'í administration and through a keener reliance on the beneficial effects of proper consultation, so that the communities they guide will reflect a pattern of life that will offer hope to the disillusioned members of society.

That there are indications that the Lesser Peace cannot be too far distant, that the local and national institutions of the Administrative Order are growing steadily in experience and influence, that the plans for the construction of the remaining administrative edifices on the Arc are in an advanced stage — that these hopeful conditions make more discernible the shaping of the dynamic synchronization envisaged by Shoghi Effendi, no honest observer can deny.

As a community clearly in the vanguard of the constructive forces at work on the planet, and as one which has access to proven knowledge, let us be about our Father's business. He will, from His glorious retreats on high, release liberal effusions of His grace upon our humble efforts, astonishing us with the incalculable victories of His conquering power. It is for the unceasing blessings of such a Father that we shall continue to supplicate on behalf of each and every one of you at the Sacred Threshold.

(Riḍván 1990 message written by the Universal House of Justice to the Bahá'ís of the world)

46.   Above all, it is essential for the friends to have the confidence that a new receptivity is dawning in the hearts of Europeans, and to have faith that the seeds they sow will germinate. They must know that the time is coming when the number of their fellow-countrymen who accept the Faith will suddenly increase, and they must be ready and eager to welcome these new believers.

(12 September 1991, written on behalf of the Universal House of Justice to a National Spiritual Assembly)

47.   All these developments have made it evident that the accumulated potential for further progress of the Bahá'í community is incalculable. The changed situation within and among nations and the many problems afflicting society amplify this potential. The impression produced by such change is of the near approach of the Lesser Peace. But there has been a simultaneous recrudescence of countervailing forces. With the fresh tide of political freedom resulting from the collapse of the strongholds of communism has come an explosion of nationalism. The concomitant rise of racism in many regions has become a matter of serious global concern. These are compounded by an upsurge in religious fundamentalism which is poisoning the wells of tolerance. Terrorism is rife. Widespread uncertainty about the condition of the economy indicates a deep disorder in the management of the material affairs of the planet, a condition which can only exacerbate the sense of frustration and futility affecting the political realm. The worsening state of the environment and of the health of huge populations is a source of alarm. And yet an element of this change is the amazing advances in communications technology making possible the rapid transmission of information and ideas from one part of the world to the other. It is against such "simultaneous processes of rise and fall, of integration and of disintegration, of order and chaos, with their continuous and reciprocal reactions on each other", that a myriad new opportunities for the next stage in the unfoldment of the beloved Master's Divine Plan present themselves.

The burgeoning influence of Bahá'u'lláh's Revelation seemed, with the imminence of the Holy Year, to have assumed the character of an onrushing wind blowing through the archaic structures of the old order, felling might pillars and clearing the ground for new conceptions of social organization. The call for unity, for a new world order, is audible from many directions. The change in world society is characterized by a phenomenal speed. A feature of this change is a suddenness, or precipitateness, which appears to be the consequence of some mysterious, rampant force. The positive aspects of this change reveal an unaccustomed openness to global concepts, movement towards international and regional collaboration, an inclination of warring parties to opt for peaceful solutions, a search for spiritual values. Even the Community of the Most Great Name itself is experiencing the rigorous effects of this quickening wind as it ventilates the modes of thought of us all, renewing, clarifying and amplifying our perspectives as to the purpose of the Order of Bahá'u'lláh in the wake of humanity's suffering and turmoil.

The situation in the world, while presenting us with an acute challenge of the utmost urgency, calls to mind the encouraging global vision of Shoghi Effendi for the prospects of the Administrative Order during the second century of the Bahá'í Era, whose midpoint we are rapidly approach. In 1946, he wrote: "The second century is destined to witness a tremendous deployment and a notable consolidation of the forces working towards the world-wide development of that Order, as well as the first stirrings of that World Order, of which the present Administrative System is at once the precursor, the nucleus and pattern — an Order which, as it slowly crystallizes and radiates its benign influence over the entire planet, will proclaim at once the coming of age of the whole human race, as well as the maturity of the Faith itself, the progenitor of that Order."

(Ridván 1992 message written by the Universal House of Justice to the
Bahá'ís of the world)

48.   The centennial year was also a period in which the situation in the world at large became more confused and paradoxical: there were simultaneous signs of order and chaos, promise and frustration. Amid the convolutions of the current global state of affairs, but with such feelings of wonder and joy, courage and faith as the Holy Year has induced in our hearts, we, at this Ridván, in the one hundred and fiftieth year of our Faith, are embarked upon a Three Year Plan. Its brevity is compelled by the swiftly changing tides of the times. But the

Plan's primary purpose is indispensable to the future of the Cause and of humankind. It is the next stage in the unfoldment of the divine charter of teaching penned by the Centre of the Covenant. The Plan will be a measure of our determination to respond to the immense opportunities at this critical moment in the social evolution of the planet. Through resolute pursuit of its stated objectives and full realization of its goals, as suited to the circumstances of each national community, the way will be made clear for a fit projection of the role of the Faith in relation to the inevitable challenges facing all humanity towards the end of the fast fleeting, fate-laden twentieth century.

A massive expansion of the Bahá'í community must be achieved far beyond all past records. The task of spreading the Message to the generality of mankind in villages, towns and cities must be rapidly extended. The need for this is critical, for without it the laboriously erected agencies of the Administrative Order will not be provided the scope to be able to develop and adequately demonstrate their inherent capacity to minister to the crying needs of humanity in its hour of deepening despair. In this regard the mutuality of teaching and administration must be fully understood and widely emphasized, for each reinforces the other. The problems of society which affect our community and those problems which naturally arise from within the community itself, whether social, spiritual, economic or administrative, will be solved as our numbers and resources multiply, and as at all levels of the community the friends develop the ability, willingness, courage and determination to obey the laws, apply the principles and administer the affairs of the Faith in accordance with divine precepts.

The new Plan revolves around a triple theme: enhancing the vitality of the faith of individual believers, greatly developing the human resources of the Cause, and fostering the proper functioning of local and national Bahá'í institutions. This is to lend focus to requisites of success as the Plan's manifold goals are pursued in these turbulent times....

Training of the friends and their striving, through serious individual study, to acquire knowledge of the Faith, to apply its principles and administer its affairs, are indispensable to developing the human resources necessary to the progress of the Cause. But knowledge alone is not adequate; it is vital that training be given in a manner that inspires love and devotion, fosters firmness in the Covenant, prompts the individual to active participation in the work of the Cause and to taking sound initiatives in the promotion of its interests. Special efforts to attract people of capacity to the Faith will also go far towards providing the human resources so greatly needed at this time. Moreover, these endeavours will stimulate and strengthen the ability of Spiritual Assemblies to meet their weighty responsibilities.

The proper functioning of these institutions depends largely on the efforts of their members to familiarize themselves with their duties and to adhere scrupulously to principle in their personal behaviour and in the conduct of their official responsibilities. Of relevant importance, too, are their resolve to remove all traces of estrangement and sectarian tendencies from their midst, their ability to win the affection and support of the friends under their care and to involve as many individuals as possible in the work of the Cause. By their constantly aiming at improving their performance, the communities they guide will reflect a pattern of life that will be a credit to the Faith and will, as a welcome consequence, rekindle hope among the increasingly disillusioned members of society.

(Ridván 1993 message written by the Universal House of Justice to the Bahá'ís of the world)

9.   It is understandable that you feel concern about methods of teaching which apply pressure to people to declare their Faith in Bahá'u'lláh, or which register as believers those who apparently have no real knowledge of the Faith or its Message....

The teaching of the Cause has always called for wisdom, devotion, enthusiasm, purity of intention and eloquence of speech. Like other human beings, Bahá'ís tend to go to extremes, and too few people bring the proper balance to the way they act. This is particularly true in the teaching of the Faith. At one extreme are those who are so on fire with the love for the Faith and with awareness of the desperate need of the people for its healing Message, that they overstep the bounds of wisdom and discretion and stray into the area of proselytizing. At the other extreme are those who are so gentle in their approach and so concerned never to arouse an adverse reaction that they fail to convey the enormous importance of the Cause or to convince their hearers; for if the messenger is not enthusiastic, how can he convey enthusiasm to others? The first extreme leads to misrepresentation of the Teachings and causes disillusionment; the second results in the stagnation of the community and its failure to fulfil its fundamental duty of conveying this life-giving Message to the world.

In this, as in all aspects of the work of the Cause, the solution lies in the friends' being patient and forbearing towards those whose shortcomings distress them, and in endeavouring, through the Assemblies' consultation, to draw closer to a proper balance while maintaining the momentum of the work and canalizing the enthusiasm of the believers.

In one of its messages, published on page 32 of "Wellspring of Guidance", the Universal House of Justice gave the following advice:

> Those who declare themselves as Bahá'ís should become enchanted with the beauty of the teachings, and touched by the love of Bahá'u'lláh. The declarants need not know all the proofs, history, laws, and principles of the Faith, but in the process of declaring themselves they must, in addition to catching the spark of faith, become basically informed about the Central Figures of the Faith, as well as the existence of laws they must follow and an administration they must obey.

In the western world in recent decades, Bahá'ís have grown used to thinking that the process by which a person accepts the Faith takes a long time, and that it is unthinkable for someone to intelligently accept Bahá'u'lláh within minutes of hearing of Him. This may be the pattern to which they have become accustomed, but it is far from being a universal one. When people accepted the Faith quickly in Africa and other parts of the Third World, western Bahá'ís sometimes explained it away by saying that such people were less educated and had fewer ideas to work their way through. Now the same process is happening in the countries of the former Eastern Bloc, and highly educated people are accepting the Faith as soon as they hear of it, embracing it enthusiastically, and rapidly deepening their understanding of its Teachings by reading every Bahá'í book they can lay their hands on. So it is clear that receptivity to spiritual truth is, as Bahá'u'lláh indicated, a matter of purity of heart, not of education or lack of it.

In the west of Europe, too, there are signs of greater receptivity towards the Faith among the people, and some are ready to join the community of the Most Great Name if approached in the proper manner. In such cases when an individual hears the Message of Bahá'u'lláh and is moved to declare his faith there should be no obstacle placed in his way. Great care must be taken that when the heart of the individual is touched by the power of Bahá'u'lláh's Message and the declarant has expressed his desire to embrace the Faith, the process of deepening be followed almost immediately. Deepening the knowledge of the new believer in the verities of the Faith is the most vital part of teaching; but deepening is not merely the imparting of knowledge — it requires also to imbue the soul of the person with the love of Bahá'u'lláh so that his faith may grow day by day and he becomes a steadfast believer.

In the following statement, Shoghi Effendi advises the Bahá'í teacher to advance the process of deepening for a person who is attracted to the Faith:

Let him [the Bahá'í teacher] consider the degree of his hearer's receptivity, and decide for himself the suitability of either the direct or indirect method of teaching, whereby he can impress upon the seeker the vital importance of the Divine Message, and persuade him to throw in his lot with those who have already embraced it. Let him remember the example set by 'Abdu'l-Bahá, and His constant admonition to shower such kindness upon the seeker, and exemplify to such a degree the spirit of the teachings he hopes to instil into him, that the recipient will be spontaneously impelled to identify himself with the Cause embodying such teachings. Let him refrain, at the outset, from insisting on such laws and observances as might impose too severe a strain on the seeker's newly awakened faith, and endeavour to nurse him, patiently, tactfully, and yet determinedly, into full maturity, and aid him to proclaim his unqualified acceptance of whatever has been ordained by Bahá'u'lláh. Let him, as soon as that stage has been attained, introduce him to the body of the fellow-believers, and seek, through constant fellowship and active participation in the local activities of his community, to enable him to contribute his share to the enrichment of its life, the furtherance of its tasks, the consolidations of its interests, and the coordination of its activities with those of its sister communities. Let him not be content until he has infused into his spiritual child so deep a longing as to impel him to arise independently, in his turn, and devote his energies to the quickening of other souls, and the upholding of the laws and principles laid down by his newly adopted Faith.

("The Advent of Divine Justice" (Wilmette: Bahá'í Publishing Trust, 1990), pp. 51-52)

From these words of the Guardian we can see that wisdom, encouragement, persuasion, and patience, are all called for, and that these must be attuned to the response shown by the hearer. We also see that the process of deepening continues long after the new believer has enrolled in the Bahá'í community.

(30 June 1993, written on behalf of the Universal House of Justice to an individual believer)

Index

Note: All numbers refer to extract numbers.